Airing cupboard ghosts
holding music practices
inside the water tank.

Television ghosts
poke crooked fingers
across your favourite programme.

Chimney ghosts
sing one-note songs
over and over in owly voices.

Vacuum-cleaner ghosts
roar and the dust obeys them,
into the bag.

But the worst ghost
hides under your bed at night.

He makes no noise at all.

Also by Irene Rawnsley

Ask A Silly Question

IRENE RAWNSLEY
DOG'S DINNER

Illustrated by Simone Abel

MAMMOTH

For Peter and Luke

First published in Great Britain 1990
by Methuen Children's Books Ltd
Published 1991 by Mammoth
an imprint of Reed Consumer Books Ltd
Michelin House, 81 Fulham Road, London SW3 6RB
and Auckland, Melbourne, Singapore and Toronto

Reprinted 1993

Text copyright © 1990 Irene Rawnsley
Illustrations copyright © 1990 Simone Abel

ISBN 0 7497 0615 5

A CIP catalogue record for this title
is available from the British Library

Printed in Great Britain
by Cox and Wyman Ltd, Reading, Berks

This paperback is sold subject to the condition
that it shall not, by way of trade or otherwise,
be lent, resold, hired out, or otherwise circulated
without the publisher's prior consent in any form
of binding or cover other than that in which
it is published and without a similar condition
including this condition being imposed
on the subsequent purchaser.

I've got a dog as thin as a rail!

Contents

Hot Sausage	1
Dog's Dinner	2
What Daniel Told Me	4
Knock-A-Door Run	6
Chickaboo	8
Caterpillars	10
Trying On	11
The Lollipop Dog	12
Bear	14
A Good Idea	16
Invisible	18
No Go	19
Grandmother's Dress	20
Crocodile Tears	22
Elephants	24
If	25
Bicycle Bones	26
The Singing Garden	28
The Wonderful Egg	29
Meeting On A Plate	30
Who Did It?	32
Snowfall	33
Dragon's Breath	34
Twin Sisters	36
Big Boots	38
The Door	39
House Ghosts	40
Don't Jump in Puddles	42
Spinning Poems	43
The End Of The World	44

New Kid on the Block
Jigsaw Bird

Hot Sausage

'Roll over!'
said the sausage,
hot from the pan;
'You chips had
better keep in line;
I'm Sausage Superman!'

Dog's Dinner

On Thursday night
my mother said
that I could sleep
in the barley sugar bed.

I dreamed of sailing
a bubble-gum boat
blown big as a dinosaur
to keep me afloat.

On Friday night
my mother said
my sister could sleep
in the barley sugar bed.

She dreamed of
a liquorice homework book
that ate the sums
when she was stuck.

On Saturday
my mother said
she would like to sleep
in the barley sugar bed.

She dreamed of
a trifle covered in cream
with lollipop spoons
to lick it clean.

When Sunday came
my mother said
the dog could sleep
on the barley sugar bed.

He ate it.

What Daniel Told Me

Daniel says
the park is spooky-woo
at night.

There's owls
tu-whit tu-whoo!
who float
the dark
to pluck you
by the hair
carry you
howling
to the tops
of trees
where ghosts
whee eee whee eee!
are hung
to freeze
your bones
with fright . . .

but Daniel says we're
all right
in the daytime.

It only
happens
at night.

Knock-A-Door Run

Come on, Lucy,
let's have fun;
let's go playing
Knock-a-door run.

This looks like
a good door to knock.

An old man comes
with a walking stick;
he's very cross
but he can't go quick;
run, Lucy, run!

Here's another door
to knock.

An old woman comes
in a purple wig;
her lap dog barks
but it's not very big;
run, Lucy, run!

Here's another door
to knock.

Oh no! IT'S A BEAR!
all teeth and claws
with rolling eyes
and swiping paws;
RUN, LUCY, RUN!

CLIMB UP THE DRAINPIPE!

Bear in the garden,
send for the zoo!
Children on the rooftop,
what can we do?

We need a ladder
but nobody will come
to help those kids
who played
Knock-a-door run.

Chickaboo

Chickaboo monkey
lived in the jungle;
climbed to the top
of a very tall tree.

Looked at the sky,
a big blue blanket;
looked at the leaves,
a big green sea;

looked at the sun,
a big orange ball
and said,

'I want the sun to play with!'

The tree shook its branches;
'No, no, no;
you've climbed as high
as a monkey can go.'

But Chickaboo
jumped high
and higher
and higher than high
till he rolled on the blanket
of the big blue sky.

He rolled to the ball
of the golden sun
and said,

'I've come to play with you.'

But the sun said,
'I've no time to play;
I'm much too busy
making day.'

Then the sun stuck out
his golden tongue
and sent little Chickaboo
rolling home.

Caterpillars

```
    er          in
  t p    s    a
 a    i   r    h
c      lla       urry
```

```
              ni          sa
               n  n     e  n
              u   g   o    d
              r      sh      socks
```

```
     to              e  l
    f  p       m    e
    f   u    o   t
   o    t  s      ters
```

```
          he           ll
         t  c       i  a
         n    a   p   r
         i       ter      box
```

Trying On

My brother's boots
are boats on me,
my sister's
are too small.

Mum's silver shoes
are far too high;
I know;
I've tried them all.

The Lollipop Dog

The lollipop dog
waits in the street
outside the shop.

He likes to eat
sweets of all sorts
for his lunch;
jelly beans,
toffee drops,
candy crunch,
but his favourite food
is a lollipop.
If you meet him
don't ever stop
to give him a snuff;
he loves
all kinds of lollipops,
can't get enough.

Never never never
give him a lick,
or you'll be left
with only a stick.

Bear

Today
I saw a bear
in a tree;

I'm sure
that bear
was watching me.

He moved,
I heard
the branches creak;

leaves blew,
I saw two
bright eyes blink.

I hurried home
to fetch my mum,
but when
she came

that bear
had gone.

A Good Idea

Today I might just make
one of my inventions.

What will you invent?

A machine to stand by the cooker
and stir the gravy.
Mum can have time off.

But who will do the vegetables?

This machine has another arm
which can peel potatoes,
chop them up
and put them in the pan.

But who will buy the potatoes?

This machine has another arm
with a basket on the end
which stretches out of the door,
down the street
and into the greengrocer's shop.

But how does it pay the shopkeeper?

You put money in the basket,
he puts in potatoes.

But what if someone steals the money?

This machine has another arm
with a policeman on the end,
carrying a truncheon.

Will it be ready by dinnertime?

No. Today I might just help mum
to make the dinner myself.

Invisible

Have you seen
Toby's invisible car?
He's lost it.

It's got no wheels,
no doors;
it isn't painted red,

no roof,
no steering wheel or seats;
that's what Toby said.

The person who
has stolen it
can't have driven far;
it's got no petrol
in the tank,
Toby's invisible car.

No Go

Our clock's lost its tick;
you can try till you're sick
   of shaking
and quaking
and rattling
and rolling
and tinkering
and tilting
and meddling
and mending
and poking
and picking
and peeking into the back;
it's been given the sack.

Pale on the mantelpiece
silent it stands,
not knowing what
to do with its hands.

Grandmother's Dress

Grandmother's flowery dress
was in bud
when she came to call
at eleven.

By afternoon
her dress
had bloomed with roses,
pinks and violets;

she blossomed
like a garden
in the chair;
her perfume filled the room.

'We're having tea
outdoors today;
will you come,
grandmother, please?'

'Oh no, my dear,
I can't do that;
I'd be bothered
by bees.'

Crocodile Tears

I used to spend
the afternoon with fishes,
come to play,
and birds would perch
upon my snout
to pass the time of day.

There was always
someone popping to the river
for a talk;
young deer,
a tender antelope,
the nicest kind of folk.

Now no one notices
my tears
are deepening the swamp;
I've got toothache
in a dozen teeth,
rheumatics from the damp.

I'm a miserable crocodile,
forgotten,
left alone;
my friends don't come
to see me
'cos I've eaten every one.

Elephants

If a hundred elephants
tried to board a bus
would the driver
make a fuss?

And if fifty elephants
came all together
to do their shopping at Tesco
would it cause
a fiasco?

And if twenty elephants
came to school
one morning
with books in their trunks
would the teacher
keep her cool?

And if one
very little elephant,
smaller than all the rest
wanted to be my friend
for just one day
would my mum
let him stay?

If

If you were
a ball of wool
I'd knit
a woolly jumper
out of you.

If you were sweets
I'd keep you
in a shiny jar
on the shelf.

If you were soap
I'd blow you
into bubbles
from my window.

If you were
my friend
we'd find
a hundred things
to do.

Bicycle Bones

Old Bones the skeleton
bought himself
a bicycle,
rode it into town
when the moon was full.

Rode it rattle-clankity,
cobblestones,
kerbstones;
all the cosy citizens
tucked up tight.

Rode it clatter-bonkity,
roadways,
railings;
gave the sleepy citizens
a sleepless night.

Rode it cockle-clunkety,
in and out
the dustbins;
rats, mice and alley cats
ran for their lives!

Old Bones the skeleton
rode his bike
like billy-ho,
up and down the tired town
all night long.

The Singing Garden

Mr. Barley next door hates birds.
He says they eat his seeds
and peck the buds from primroses
before they've time to bloom.

He's made jam jar traps,
put bottles on sticks,
hung shiny silver tops
and strings of tin cans
across his vegetable patch,
to scare them.

Strong winds blowing
make music in Mr. Barley's garden.
Birds come from miles away
to sit on the roof and listen.

The Wonderful Egg

This morning
from my breakfast egg
grew a twig.

From the twig
grew a leaf;
from the leaf
grew a tree.

From the tree
came a sea;
from the sea
came an oar:

Now I'm afloat
in an eggshell boat,
looking for the shore.

Meeting On A Plate

A snail met a worm
on a lettuce leaf
in a plateful of salad
one day.

They agreed
that the world
is a wonderful place;
'So green,'
said the worm.
'So cool,'
said the snail
as they nibbled
a cucumber slice.

They slid
along celery,
tasted tomatoes;
'So soft,'
said the snail;
'So wet,'
said the worm,
and they travelled
a watercress stalk,

happily talking;
until up above them
somebody lifted
a big knife and fork.

Who Did It?

Who put pudding
in dad's best black shoes?

Me.

Who put jelly
in his umbrella?

Me.

Who put a spider
in his bowler hat
and stuffed his briefcase
full of old comics?

Me.

Then go to bed
without any tea.

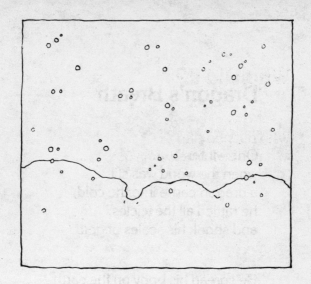

Snowfall

Snow fell
like burglar's footfalls
in the night;

borders,
paths,
lawn,
paving
were covered
all in white;

snow stole
the garden
while we slept last night.

Dragon's Breath

One winter
when the world was still
a dragon came into the cold;
he rattled all the icicles
and shook his scales of gold.

He spread his body on the earth
to make the flowers grow;
he snorted
with his fiery breath
and melted all the snow.

He snorted
with his fiery breath
to set the river free;
he coiled his golden tail
around a budding hazel tree.

He coiled his golden tail
until catkins began to shake,
then spread his wings
and flew
to warm another world awake.

Twin Sisters

My sisters
are pictures in a pop-up book,
only made of cardboard
if you care to look.

Visitors
admire their lacy dresses,
matching noses,
curly tresses;

but if nobody's looking
the smiles fold down
into twin, mean faces,
sulky frowns.

They're pop-up pictures,
I'm sure of that.
I'd like to shut the pages
and squash them flat.

Big Boots

Suppose I wore
size ninety-nine boots,
I'd walk in mud
wherever I found it.

I'd make
a trail of footprints
down the street
so that people
would say,
'Let's hurry away;
a giant
or a monster
or a yeti
or a dinosaur
or a great big
hairy gorilla
came this way!'

I'd keep my boots
in the garden shed,
and hang my big feet
out of bed.

The Door

Once in a field
there stood a door;
nobody knew
what the door
was for.

It didn't have a number
or a name;
it had no letterbox;
the postman
never came.

It wasn't in a wall,
a house or hut;
there was
just a door
and the door was shut.

Old folk, young,
everybody
came to look,
but nobody dared go
knock
knock
knock.

House Ghosts

Airing cupboard ghosts
hold music practices
inside the water tank.

Television ghosts
poke crooked fingers
across your favourite programme.

Chimney ghosts
sing one-note songs
over and over in owly voices.

Vacuum-cleaner ghosts
roar and the dust obeys them,
into the bag.

But the worst ghost
hides under your bed at night.

He makes no noise at all.

Don't Jump in Puddles

'Don't jump
in puddles,'
said Samantha's mum;
'Remember
you're wearing
a new cardigan,
best blouse,
velvet dungarees,
pink socks,
white shoes
tied up with bows.'

But Samantha forgot,
and she ruined the lot.

Spinning Poems

Poems
are like tops;
you learn how
to spin them;

words become
magic circles;
you hear them
humming.

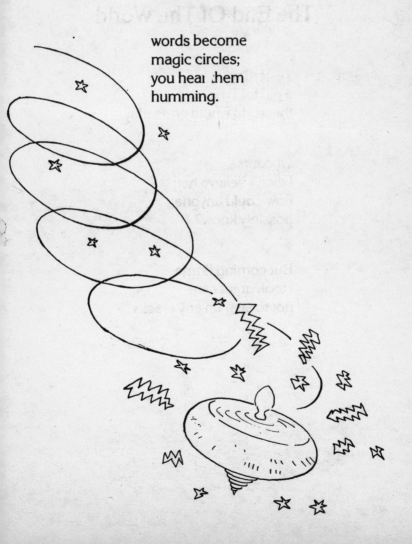

The End Of The World

Yesterday
a girl told me
the world would end today.

Of course,
I didn't believe her;
how could anyone
possibly know?

But coming home
I took great care
not to step on any cracks.

Also by Irene Rawnsley

ASK A SILLY QUESTION

*Every time
The wind is high,
Terry Ashworth
Tries to fly.*

*But although
We all of us
Give him space,
And he travels
At a terrific pace.*

*He always stays
With his feet
On the ground;
He says it's his boots
That hold him down.*

A crazy collection of poems, guaranteed to make you laugh!

Mark Burgess

CAN'T GET TO SLEEP

A sparkling collection of verse by the popular author of *Feeling Beastly*.

*Up above, the stars
are twinkling,
Hundreds, thousands,
Quite a sprinkling.
Just how many?
I've no inkling,
That's what little me is thinking.*

Mark Burgess

FEELING BEASTLY

*I love to see the jigsaw bird
Flying upside down.
It sings a song that sounds all wrong
And wears a dressing gown.*

*I love to see the sawjig bird
Flying downside up.
It feeds on chips and concrete mix
And drinks them from a cup.*

**This anthology is bursting at the seams
with beastly poems!**

William Cole and Tomi Ungerer

*BEASTLY BOYS AND
GHASTLY GIRLS*

*Speak roughly to your little boy,
And beat him when he sneezes:
He only does it to annoy,
Because he knows it teases.*
                              Lewis Carroll

A selection of funny, absurd, and truly ridiculous rhymes accompanied by hilarious drawings – guaranteed to make you giggle.

William Cole and Tomi Ungerer

OH, THAT'S RIDICULOUS!

*I've got a dog as thin as a rail,
He's got fleas all over his tail;
Every time his tail goes flop,
The fleas on the bottom all hop to the top.*

More funny, absurd and truly ridiculous rhymes from the team that brought you *Beastly Boys and Ghastly Girls, Oh, How Silly!* and *Oh, What Nonsense!*

Jennifer Curry (editor)

DOVE ON THE ROOF

Bombshell

*Last night
Bombs fell,
Tonight
Like a bombshell
Fell peace.*

Janis Priestley

A strong and moving collection of seventy-two poems that celebrate peace. Many of the poems are by children as well as great poets of the past and present, among them Thomas Hardy, Siegfried Sassoon, John Agard and Joan Aiken.

Jennifer Curry won the 1991 Earthworm Award for her anthology *The Last Rabbit*.

Jennifer Curry (editor)

THE LAST RABBIT

A collection of green poems.

The natural world is beautiful. The natural world is threatened. Here are poems to celebrate the beauty and cry out against its destruction.

THE TIGER

The tiger has wise eyes.
He knows about men.
They put traps to kill him.
They will take his coat for
rich ladies to wear.
The tiger is angry.
So am I.

Vorakit Boonchareon

Jack Prelutsky

SOMETHING BIG HAS BEEN HERE

Something big has been here,
what it was, I do not know,
for I did not see it coming,
and I did not see it go,
but I hope I never meet it,
if I do, I'm in a fix,
for it left behind its footprints,
they are size nine-fifty-six.

Two hundred wonderfully funny and inventive poems featuring various weird and wonderful characters such as Wunk the Wizard, Densom Dumm, the woolly Wurbbe and Kevin the King of the Jungle.

By the author of *The New Kid on the Block*.

'... lively and fresh."
Times Educational Supplement

'... one of the world's masters of light verse."
Junior Bookshelf

Adrian Henri

THE PHANTOM LOLLIPOP LADY
and other poems

A sparkling collection of poems especially for children by one of Britain's best-known poets.

'A new collection of poems is like a box of assorted chocolates . . . Adrian Henri's new collection is a very tasty selection. Open this tempting book yourselves and pick out your best ones . . .'

Adele Geras

'A terrific read'

Parents

Adrian Henri

RHINESTONE RHINO

A new collection of poems from the celebrated poet and performer, following on from the success of *The Phantom Lollipop Lady*. Meet a Rhino country star from Gnashville, a cow that commutes to the city in a suit, a Wartime child and a mysterious green light . . .

Funny, eerie and thoughtful, *Rhinestone Rhino* has something for everyone.

Julie Park

MORE GIGGLY RHYMES

Do cheetahs ever tell lies?
Who is Holly that eats flies?
Why's the rhino on Sam's head sat?
And where's the cat going to get a hat?

Does the farrier's daughter ever get wed?
Why is the Welsh dragon sick in his bed?
What happened to the wizard with the lizard
from his spell?

All the answers to these questions are inside
with more as well!

A beautifully illustrated picture book, the follow up to the hugely successful *GIGGLY RHYMES*.

Jack Prelutsky

THE NEW KID ON THE BLOCK

*Its fangs were red with bloody gore,
its eyes were red with menace,
it battered down my bedroom door,
and burst across my bedroom floor,
and with a loud, resounding roar
said, "ANYONE FOR TENNIS?"*

There are over a hundred witty and whacky poems to choose from in this bumper collection of verse by one of America's best-selling children's poets, Jack Prelutsky. Meet Zany Zapper Zocke, the greatest ace of videospace, Euphonica Jarre, the world's worst singer, and find out why you shouldn't quarrel with a shark!

". . . one of the world's masters of light verse."

Junior Bookshelf

A Selected List of Fiction from Mammoth

While every effort is made to keep prices low, it is sometimes necessary to increase prices at short notice. Mammoth Books reserves the right to show new retail prices on covers which may differ from those previously advertised in the text or elsewhere.

The prices shown below were correct at the time of going to press.

☐	7497 0366 0	**Dilly the Dinosaur**	Tony Bradman £1.99
☐	7497 0021 1	**Dilly and the Tiger**	Tony Bradman £1.99
☐	7497 0137 4	**Flat Stanley**	Jeff Brown £1.99
☐	7497 0048 3	**Friends and Brothers**	Dick King-Smith £1.99
☐	7497 0054 8	**My Naughty Little Sister**	Dorothy Edwards £1.99
☐	416 86550 X	**Cat Who Wanted to go Home**	Jill Tomlinson £1.99
☐	7497 0166 8	**The Witch's Big Toe**	Ralph Wright £1.99
☐	7497 0218 4	**Lucy Jane at the Ballet**	Susan Hampshire £2.25
☐	416 03212 5	**I Don't Want To!**	Bel Mooney £1.99
☐	7497 0030 0	**I Can't Find It!**	Bel Mooney £1.99
☐	7497 0032 7	**The Bear Who Stood on His Head**	W. J. Corbett £1.99
☐	416 10362 6	**Owl and Billy**	Martin Waddell £1.75
☐	416 13822 5	**It's Abigail Again**	Moira Miller £1.75
☐	7497 0031 9	**King Tubbitum and the Little Cook**	Margaret Ryan £1.99
☐	7497 0041 6	**The Quiet Pirate**	Andrew Matthews £1.99
☐	7497 0064 5	**Grump and the Hairy Mammoth**	Derek Sampson £1.99

All these books are available at your bookshop or newsagent, or can be ordered direct from the publisher. Just tick the titles you want and fill in the form below.

Mandarin Paperbacks, Cash Sales Department, PO Box 11, Falmouth, Cornwall TR10 9EN.

Please send cheque or postal order, no currency, for purchase price quoted and allow the following for postage and packing:

UK   80p for the first book, 20p for each additional book ordered to a maximum charge of £2.00.

BFPO   80p for the first book, 20p for each additional book.

Overseas   £1.50 for the first book, £1.00 for the second and 30p for each additional book
including Eire   thereafter.

NAME (Block letters) ....

ADDRESS ....

....

....